MALCOLM McLAREN

INTERVIEWED AT
THE EAGLE GALLERY
LONDON 1996

MALCOLM McLAREN INTERVIEW

Malcolm McLaren: ... down memory lane.
Because you reinvent it now, as people will
always now read into it things that you weren't
necessarily always conscious of when you did it,
the result being that they start to take on another
aspect. Here, all put up nicely in white frames,
they take on a different kind of resonance than
perhaps they did when they were sold as clothes
in a store on the King's Road and/or existed
as fly-posters like a million others out there on
the streets. Utterly disposable, certainly never
considered collectible in their day, but that's
because the creator doesn't always think what we
do is necessarily that significant at the time.

But you had an art school background?

Yeah, yeah, oh yeah, yeah. But you know, the Sixties was never about collecting anything, it was always about destroying everything, because you never really sensed any kind of career aspect in your life. We were much more interested in absolute failure, because we were ultimate, unquestionable romantics, outlaws. We were much more interested in the life of the irrational than the pragmatic and therefore never really concerned oneselves with building a future, building a career, being part of any tradition: in fact, quite the opposite.

But now, in retrospect, can you place this work as something that could be part of art history?

Well, they look very strange to me only because, being in frames on a wall, they certainly become historic, remnants of a moment in history, and in that respect they become a bit anthropological. Whether they could be considered art, I suspect they can. They're 'art-e-facts'. They're 'art-e-facts', you know. So maybe they can be considered art too because they did fulfil a moment in the cultural history of this country.

What were your influences, which artists... ?

I was no different from most people really, I don't think. Obviously, all the mystery and the lives, rather than the products of all those Dadaistic and Surrealistic painters who you honestly believed were totally into having a good time, and more interested in changing life than actually practising any art necessarily, unless their art was to do with changing life and often that meant creating events in the street. You were ultimately fascinated, and ultimately very very inspired by their lives. And later on I guess those that sort of took on their mantle after the War in the Fifties, particularly in Paris, those that were under the Gaullist mandate in Paris after the War; those that created, I suppose, rebellious angst; those that left home to discuss the politics of boredom in all those cafés on the Boulevard Saint-Germain and so on, and I suppose gave rise to a movement known as the Existentialists.

They were artistically for us inspiring. I say 'us': art students were hipper than thou in the Sixties and they were as equally interested in dealing with nihilism as a very positive lifestyle and

NO FUTURE

Maximum Penalty £5

Sex Pistols

we associated their activities with the activities of the Surrealists and the Dadaists. And, later on in the late Sixties, that all culminated for us in the most fantastic and flamboyant event that seemed engineered or inspired by the children of those Existentialists, or let's say the follow-up: the Situationists. I wouldn't say they were a movement as such; they were an artistic group of disenfranchised creatures of the art world who really were very very conscious, back in the late Fifties, of the commodification of the planet. And I suppose in a way everything that they said and debated endlessly and tried to, in their own manner, articulate – in the form of happenings, situations, occasional events, live events – did in a way for me by the mid-Seventies have an immense impact. Because having inherited their thoughts, I actually noticed them coming true before one's very eyes. I think a certain anger produced a reaction that allowed me to be anti the commodity on the King's Road in Chelsea, anti the fashion, anti the pop music, anti all established values in that regard, and anti the career and produced the anti-group of all time at that time, the Sex Pistols, and produced the most anti-fashion which is kind of what you see around you now.

**These are also works resulting from
close collaboration, how... under what
circumstances... ?**

Well, Vivienne was a primary school teacher,
and extremely conservative, and she had a
rationale from the north of England that I never
really endeared myself to, but she was my
girlfriend, and I was a virgin, and she was my
first girlfriend, and I adored her for all those
reasons. She was incredibly incredibly good with
her hands. She was a wonderful – not architect
– just a very very good artisan and I really was
one of those terrible spoilt brats of London that
couldn't be bothered with any artisanship, one of
these sort of dreamers. But you couldn't continue
to dream, you needed people to carry out the
ideas, and Vivienne was phenomenally good at
doing that.

From the little that I knew – because I came from
a tradition of the rag trade, and I had learnt to cut
and sew clothes from the age of seven onwards
– I was able to fill Vivienne up with those basic
tools of a trade, which was fashion after all at the
end of the day. But to create the kind of clothes

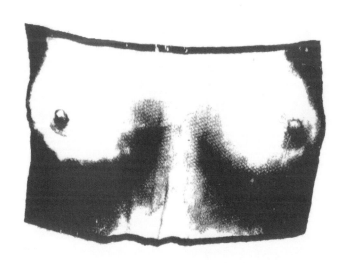

that we did, she had to understand the notion of destroying things and that was something, I guess, she semi-understood and certainly understood enough, or was willing enough to understand because I was her boyfriend. So philosophically she went along with it, encouraged really by, I guess, my passion. And that spilled over into some of the students that I picked up with again, slightly later on, during the course of having created this group, the Sex Pistols. And one of those persons was Jamie Reid, although I had absolutely nothing to do with him in art school, I thought he was a right idiot. He used to sort of paint pebbles with Druid motifs that I had, for the life of me, not in any way, any shape or form, a relationship with, and I thought it was all a bit hippy-dippy and not really where I was thinking.

However, Jamie had, during the course of the four or five years I am talking about, somehow suddenly become this printer for Situationist literature. I was quite amazed by it when I met up with him again – not by accident; he just happened to come to a Sex Pistols show. His girlfriend seemed incredibly intelligent. Her name was Sophie, and I was looking for a secretary and she seemed intelligent and clever, and very capable, and I was looking for someone just like that. And so, without hesitation, I employed her, and in doing so I suspect I picked up on this relationship with Jamie.

Jamie, having been a printer, seemed to be an absolute perfect candidate to print for me various leaflets and different things, and obviously with the Sex Pistols, that kind of artwork, and that's what he really wanted to do. He allowed me actually to promote that aspect of an anti-group that otherwise – and it's always difficult to know now – I may not have done in quite the same way. I may not have done it with quite the same commitment. I think it's a strange thing, having people who understand your past and your references and where you come from and bring them all together in a kind of gang in the Seventies, although we were Sixties children. With that in mind, you need luck to make things happen and Jamie was very much part of that plan, that fantastic thing of picking up on people who really are with a particular programme that you knew at that point in a way would definitely leave sufficient debris in its wake to, well, to never be forgotten basically. I think that was very special and very unique.

We had little, if any, true knowledge of the other generation, the generation that you see sometimes here, like Sid and so on. We didn't really understand them, but I'm not sure whether it really mattered. We just understood what we wanted to do. We were filled with immense anger and they were a perfect means – to be used – to exploit that anger. Whether they understood where we were coming from or not, I don't know. Probably I'd say not. I don't think the Sex Pistols understood ever who the Sex Pistols really were. I don't think any of their fans half-understood it, but I think they picked up on some of it. Those at a distance probably picked up on more of it, because they were able to look at it all as some extraordinary spectacle and explosion. And it's always after the fact that you can begin to enjoy these things, because you can look deeply into them and recognise that this wasn't arbitrary but that there was some mind going on.

They are not posters to sell anything. That's the most extraordinary thing. If we wanted posters to sell, we would never have done things like this. They were only there in order not to sell things. They were there to upset. They were there to

constantly remind anybody in the industry of pop culture that we were absolutely against it.

But then were you surprised when the whole thing did take off?

No, I wasn't surprised. I was more aghast at the fact that people were so thrilled by you being so anti. I was aghast. I was amazed. It was beyond being surprised. It was like, it actually gave you, not permission, but ultimately it gave you a sort of feeling that anything was possible and unquestionably you never even had to dream of the word compromise on any level. It was absolutely irrelevant in your conversations with anyone. It was this, or it was nothing, and that was it. I think that went down even to the extent of the group themselves as individuals and so on. One was naturally going to be hated at some point, and one naturally was. It was a culmination at the end. You could say one was a dictator, but I think that, yes: we were very artistic dictators.

**You had this whole 'anti' attitude, but
behind that was there also a perversity or
contradiction in wanting some ideal to exist
as well?**

Well, I think there's a perverse thing, always.
I mean if you look at everything, I would say
more or less everything around you here in this
room, you realise, it's all an absolutely vivid and
sexy enjoyment in failure. You wanted so much
to fail but in the most spectacular way humanly
possible, and if you look around you, everything
is all... you are constantly conscious of wanting to
fail. When I say that, everything around here, you
can see that's what it's all about. It's not about
self-promotion.

If you like, culture today is 100% about self-
promotion from start to finish. It is as the
Situationists say, the ultimate commodification.
All art today is a commodity, more or less. It
doesn't matter whether it's Sarah Lucas or Francis
Bacon. Probably Francis Bacon is a little less of
a commodity than Sarah Lucas, and obviously
a better artist in my opinion because of it.
However, if you look around here, none of this

is about self-promotion. It seems on the surface that ultimately self-promotion is all it's about. That's the trick. It looks on the surface as if all it's about is self-promotion, but underneath it's about celebrating a flamboyant failure in the most spectacular manner. For me, that was our artistic statement, that was our statement of intent. That was our contribution, if you like, to the culture of that time. That's when we became, for a moment, artists.

What it means is never getting off the train, never really ever ever wanting to arrive anywhere. It means never really having a destination. You know, 'Nowhere', 'Boredom', like in that poster. 'Holidays in the Sun'. It's all about never really having a holiday, except in other people's misery. It's forever wanting to be Artful Dodgers, because we kind of thought the only thing in terms of pop culture that had any sign of interest for us was to be an Artful Dodger, and who runs Artful Dodgers? Fagins. For us that was pop culture. There wasn't anything else in it. Whether it's guys telling you everything is 'all played out', sort of hanging, with nothing on from their waist down.

Whether it's de-mystifying the swastika, and showing you … Understand one thing, darling, you know: fashion. The military, the army understand more about fashion than John Galliano will ever understand about fashion. Fashion is a uniform. Fashion is fascism. Fashion is about elitism. Fashion is about class. Fashion is understood by the military. You know, the boy in the uniform. They understood what fashion is about in the military, very very very very well. It's why General de Gaulle was never out of uniform. It's why all those Latin American guys constantly decorate themselves up as dictators. Understand it's all about class – a uniform – looking better than the guy or the girl next door.

The Nazis we all know had the best clothes sense. They had the best designed uniforms. They understood more about fashion than probably any other regime or military army. They did it better than anyone else and their icon was the swastika. So it's a question of reclaiming that and turning it on its head and trying to demystify it, prettify it, put it into colours that weren't necessarily the colours that it was associated with – and destroy it. Here's the word,

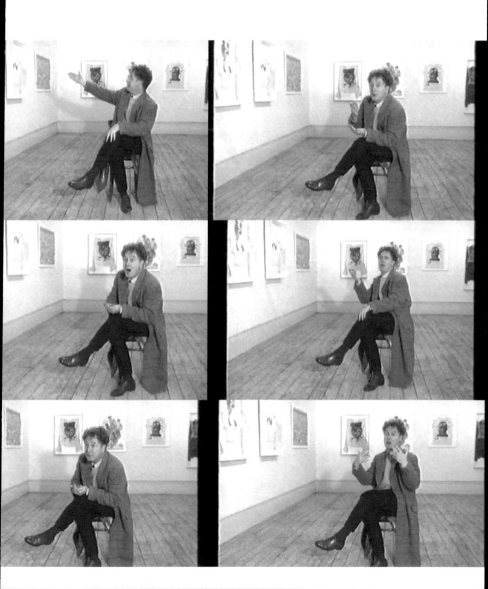

'Destroy', and what do we put with it? Well, all the other fashionable icons, the things that little sweet virginal Catholic girls wear round their neck. Jesus Christ, on the crucifix, and the things that you are always licking, the neck, the back of the Queen, every day. So, cut the head, take those icons and destroy them, that for us was an anti-fashion statement.

What was your thinking behind representing Brian Epstein alongside the Cambridge Rapist? Was that anything to do with yourself?

Well, Brian Epstein, yeah, it does in a way. At the time many many police were always investigating in my shop for the whereabouts of what they thought was this mad rapist running around Cambridge, because the one thing they understood was that he always wore this leather mask, and they thought perhaps I was the person responsible for selling him this leather mask. Well, maybe I was. I don't know or I didn't know at the time. The one thing I did know of course, was that there were about twenty other people from Cambridge including dons from the University who were all buying these leather masks. So, what

was I going to do, I thought, as a haberdasher on the King's Road, I couldn't reveal... It's a bit like one's taken a haberdasher's oath – like a Hippocratic oath – so you can't reveal the whereabouts of these chaps who want to buy leather gags and masks and do whatever they want to do in the privacy of their home or behind locked doors. I didn't really feel I wanted to reveal because I liked to protect clandestine environments, being anarchic in that kind of way.

Instead, I decided to create a T-shirt about the Cambridge Rapist and that's what that's about and associated him with the Beatles, because I had recently heard stories about Brian Epstein. How I learnt all this I don't know, but there were enough fashion victims and rock'n'roll victims on the streets of the King's Road to always share a drink with and hear them rumbling in the corner of the store about something or other, and one picked up all this nonsensical, but sometimes interesting, information.

One such story was that Brian Epstein had not died by simple suicide but had died as a result of some severe S&M practice. Well, the reason they knew of this was because he had various boyfriends that he would go and visit in the bushes of Holland Park and was always running around to various meetings, be it at EMI or wherever, often on a Monday morning, with giant bruises on his face, and cuts and so on. Apparently rather than declare this affair of that nature when the police arrived at his house, it was considered something that they would rather not talk about because I suppose The Beatles had been given an OBE by then; I suppose because they didn't really want to at that time. It was considered far too scandalous, even then. Homosexuality was still a very very very frowned-upon activity in the English system and rather than talk about all of that, they preferred to just give a verdict of suicide. So I thought, in the Seventies at that time making a T-shirt about such activities could be associated in some way with the activities of this so-called Cambridge Rapist. That's it.

Can you trace a direct influence of the punk movement on contemporary art?

Well, I do. I don't think I could ever have been party to it. I don't think Jamie could ever have

done half of it. I don't think it could have ever come about had we not been art students in the Sixties, but I don't know whether it's art. It might be bigger than art really, because art has been defined today as not much more than a commodity and I don't think these things really are. I think they remain even now, even set up in frames as artefacts, they still seem fairly enigmatic. They still escape you somewhat and there's a lot about it and maybe just in these frames, they do that more than ever. I don't know, and you could say, as I said earlier, they are just memories, but... it's when you look at them and think, why on earth would anyone, or what were those people that wore them? Why would anyone want to wear them? And yet I suppose you feel, or I would feel, that that's not the point.

The point is they are statements of intent at a time that no one thought possible that you could make a statement about fashion that was not fashion. That you could use fashion just as you could use music to create a point of view that surpassed all music or fashion, that was just the carrier, and in a sense that maybe makes them art. It might well do. It's a difficult question. I look at them and

I think in some respects they have much more provenance than a lot of things in galleries today that would be considered contemporary art, but only because maybe all things in galleries today, more often than not English things, seem to be the children of some of these things funnily enough. So I think that this is the precursor, this is maybe the origins, of a lot of things you see in British contemporary art today.

Can you give some examples of what you mean?

Well, I saw a huge exhibition at the Musée d'Art Moderne de la Ville de Paris which was called 'Live Art' or 'Live Life' or 'Life Live'. It was full of installations by various known British artists, the Chapman brothers for instance. It was all a contemporary British art show. It featured films by Douglas Gordon. It featured photographs by – God, what's her name? Jesus, I can't remember, but she's the girlfriend of Jay Jopling, but I can't remember her name. There was stuff by Sarah Lucas, stuff by Angus Fairhurst, Damien Hirst. I guess if these people weren't artists, they might have been in punk rock bands. They might have been very good at being in punk rock bands. They all seem to be kind of punk rock artists in a way. I don't think people like to use that term because that term is such a term invented by the media and people have a sufficient amount of ego to want to be known as artists. They don't want anything else attached to them – maybe the word 'contemporary', I don't know – and they are right in that respect.

I must say that this, what you see around you, was never called punk by me. It was never called punk rock.

It was always an art thing.

It always was.

AFTERWORDS

When I first met Malcolm McLaren in March 1998,
I knew very little about him. I didn't know about
his work in fashion and that his roots lay in that
world. His mother had had a successful dress
factory in East London called Eve Edwards, and
his grandfather was a master tailor on Savile
Row. Malcolm knew everything about clothes.
His technical knowledge was astonishing and
his conceptual and stylistic abilities were
unparalleled.

This background coupled with his art school
education led him to create a new kind of
Gesamtkunstwerk with his shops at 430 King's
Road (possibly the world's first pop-up shops):
Let It Rock, Too Fast To Live Too Young To Die,
Sex, Seditionaries, Worlds End, and lastly, at
5 St Christopher's Place, Nostalgia of Mud.

Each shop was a living installation with a unique
concept devised by Malcolm that was expressed

in its philosophy, exterior, interior, graphics, music and wares – the fashion, which he created with the help of his then-girlfriend, Vivienne Westwood. (The corresponding music went from records in the jukebox to his managing the Sex Pistols and Bow Wow Wow and finally becoming a musical artist in his own right.)

This all brought together his life-long obsession, 'The look of music and the sound of fashion.' Because everything was created as a pure artistic expression, the results were powerful and revolutionary. Only because he knew so much about fashion could he destroy and deconstruct them into an artwork – a kind of wearable collage. As Malcolm explained, 'This wasn't fashion as a commodity. This was fashion as an idea.'

When I visited Malcolm at his home in London, he showed me two framed pieces: a T-shirt and a handkerchief. He explained, with pleased wonderment, that some people had collected his early clothes and exhibited them as artworks in frames.

Later, I discovered he meant Paul Stolper and Andrew Wilson. I am grateful for what they have done, in recognising the importance of this work and documenting and preserving it.

Young Kim

This interview with Malcolm McLaren took place
at the Eagle Gallery in 1996 during the exhibition
*"I groaned with pain" – Sex, Seditionaries and
the Sex Pistols*, curated by Paul Stolper and
Andrew Wilson. For the first time the visual
'debris' of the Sex Pistols – graphics by Jamie
Reid and Helen Wellington-Lloyd, and clothes
by Malcolm McLaren and Vivienne Westwood
– was presented as the product of a complex
collaborative art practice. The exhibition was
visited by many artists and critics associated with
the generation of young British artists (YBAs)
who were coming to the fore at that time and
were alluded to by McLaren at the end of his
interview. Following this exhibition, elements
of the Stolper Wilson collection, as it became
known, were exhibited widely – nationally
and internationally – and in 2004 and 2005 the
majority of the collection was exhibited at The
Hospital in London and Urbis in Manchester,
and documented in the accompanying book

No Future: Sex, Seditionaries and the Sex Pistols with texts by Michael Bracewell and Andrew Wilson. The collection as a whole has now been dispersed. In 2018 the clothes were acquired by the Costume Institute at the Metropolitan Museum of Art in New York. In 2022, the graphic element of the collection was sold in a single-owner auction by Sotheby's.

Andrew Wilson

PICTURES:

Page 6: Back cover of the catalogue to the exhibition *"I groaned with pain" – Sex, Seditionaries and the Sex Pistols*, Eagle Gallery 1996, reproducing Jamie Reid *No Future* sticker 1977.

Page 9: Front cover of the catalogue to the exhibition *"I groaned with pain" – Sex, Seditionaries and the Sex Pistols*, Eagle Gallery 1996, reproducing detail of Malcolm McLaren and Vivienne Westwood, *Tits* T-shirt design (detail), Sex/Seditionaries 1975-1979.

Page 22: Malcolm McLaren and Vivienne Westwood, *Destroy* muslin shirt, Seditionaries 1977 (Stolper Wilson Collection 1993-2018, exhibited Eagle Gallery 1996)

Page 24: (top): Malcolm McLaren and Vivienne Westwood, *Two Cowboys* T-shirt, SEX c. 1974-5 (Stolper Wilson Collection 1993-2018, exhibited Eagle Gallery 1996)

Page 24: (bottom) Malcolm McLaren and Vivienne Westwood, *Oliver Twist/Cruikshank* muslin shirt, Seditionaries 1978 (Stolper Wilson Collection 1993-2018, exhibited Eagle Gallery 1996)

Page 27: Malcolm McLaren and Vivienne Westwood, *Cambridge Rapist* T-shirt, Seditionaries 1978 (Stolper Wilson Collection 1993-2018, exhibited Eagle Gallery 1996)

Published by Stolper Wilson © 2023
with thanks to Young Kim and the Estate of Malcolm McLaren
Designed by Damian Jaques 8Books.co.uk
Produced by Mark Fletcher fletcherbooks.org
ISBN: 978-1-9160233-5-2
Printed and bound in the UK by Pureprint

MIX
Supporting responsible forestry
FSC® C022913
www.fsc.org

The publishers would like to thank Emma Hill, Simon Turnbull, Anna Hugo and Ingrid Swenson.